THE GREAT EASTERN MAIN LINE

LONDON LIVERPOOL STREET–NORWICH

Adam Head

AMBERLEY

This book is dedicated in loving memory to Patricia Ann Blower
1939–2019
Heaven's gain is truly Earth's loss.

First published 2019

Amberley Publishing
The Hill, Stroud
Gloucestershire, GL5 4EP

www.amberley-books.com

ISBN 978 1 4456 9267 8 (print)
ISBN 978 1 4456 9268 5 (ebook)

British Library Cataloguing in Publication Data.
A catalogue record for this book is available from the British Library.

Typesetting by Aura Technology and Software Services, India. Printed in UK.

Contents

Introduction

Extending for 114 miles, the Great Eastern Main Line connects East Anglia to the capital, running from Norwich to London Liverpool Street through Norfolk, Suffolk and Essex. Passengers using the Great Eastern Main Line (GEML) can reach the capital in roughly two hours, the main stations on the Great Eastern Main Line are:

- Norwich
- Diss
- Stowmarket
- Needham Market
- Ipswich
- Manningtree
- Colchester
- Marks Tey
- Kelvedon
- Witham
- Hatfield Peverel
- Chelmsford
- Ingatestone
- Shenfield
- Brentwood
- Harold Wood
- Gidea Park
- Romford
- Chadwell Heath
- Goodmayes
- Seven Kings
- Ilford
- Manor Park
- Forest Gate
- Maryland
- Stratford
- London Liverpool Street

The fourteen stations from Shenfield to London Liverpool Street make up part of the Metro services that run every fifteen minutes between Shenfield and London Liverpool Street, operated by TfL Rail.

At the north end of the Great Eastern Main Line, over 100 miles away from London Liverpool Street, is the very attractive station of Norwich. After travelling on the Great Eastern Main Line passengers can change here for Abellio Greater Anglia connections to Cambridge, Great Yarmouth, Lowestoft and Sheringham , as well as East Midlands Trains connections to Peterborough, the Midlands and the North.

The Greater Anglia logo, as seen on a Class 90.

GEML History

The Great Eastern Main Line was opened in 1862 and has seen a variety of different traction providing the Norwich–London Liverpool Street services, with British Railways Standard Class 7 steam engines providing the traction before British Railways pulled the plug on steam-hauled services in the late 1960s. Later came the Class 40 diesel locomotive, which were later replaced by the Class 47 diesel locomotive that, with a maximum speed of 95 mph and rapid acceleration, proved to be very popular.

The pioneer of the Class 90 fleet, No. 90001 sits at Norwich with a service for London Liverpool Street. This loco is called *Crown Point* in recognition of the depot just outside Norwich station.

The Great Eastern Main Line was electrified in the 1950s as far as Colchester before being fully electrified in the 1980s; Ipswich in the early 1980s and the final part to Norwich in 1986. When Norwich wasn't electrified and the Class 86 electric locomotive was starting to take over the Norwich–London duties from the Class 47s, Class 86 locos would operate the London to Ipswich section of the line before allowing the Class 47 to take over for the final part to Norwich. After 1986 the Class 86 did the entire journey from Norwich to London Liverpool Street.

These Class 86s stayed on the Great Eastern Main Line in the era of privatisation when the Great Eastern Main Line was taken over by Anglia Railways in 1997, taking over from InterCity (a division of British Railways). This resulted in the stock of Class 86s, British Railways Mk 2 carriages and driving brake standard open (DBSO) being repainted from their recognisable InterCity livery into new turquoise Anglia Railways livery.

Towards the end of the Anglia Railways franchise in 2004, the organisation started looking at the feasibility of replacing the elderly Class 86 locomotives with Class 90 locomotives, and Freightliner Class 90s starting to appear on Norwich–London services. In 2004 Anglia Railways lost their franchise and National Express became the new owners of the Great Eastern Main Line, with their odd choice for a franchise name (ONE) confusing passengers. They replaced all the Class 86s, Mk 2 carriages and DBSOs with Class 90 electric locomotives, Mk 3 carriages and driving van trailers (DVT), which made the services faster and able to carry more passengers.

In 2012 National Express lost their franchise to the current owners of the Great Eastern Main Line, Abellio Greater Anglia, who have kept the current stock running after ten years. The stock is due to be replaced in the future as, after more than fifty years, loco-hauled trains on the Great Eastern Main Line will be replaced with electric multiple units.

Present Day Trains on the GEML

The Great Eastern Main Line has a wide variety of trains operating on all areas. There are a wide variety of units, as well as the loco-hauled services that run between Norwich and London Liverpool Street. Although diesel multiple units (DMUs) stopped operating south of Ipswich, apart from the non-electrified branch line from Marks Tey to Sudbury, the following trains can be seen on the Great Eastern Main Line.

Class 153 Sprinter diesel multiple units

These one-carriage 75-mph units were converted from Class 155 diesel multiple units to one-carriage trains in 1991/92 and are operated solely by Abellio Greater Anglia. They are primarily used on the Felixstowe and the Sudbury lines but have been known to make appearances on the Bury St Edmunds line to both Cambridge and Peterborough and the East Suffolk line to Lowestoft. Abellio Greater Anglia own five Class 153 Sprinters – 153306, 153309, 153314, 153322 and 153335. When these units aren't working out of Ipswich they can be seen north working in and out of Norwich.

Class 153 Sprinter diesel multiple unit No. 153306 sits at Ipswich with a service for Felixstowe.

Class 156 Sprinter diesel multiple unit No. 156409 sits at Norwich with a service for Sheringham.

Class 156 Sprinter diesel multiple units

These two 75-mph carriage units built between 1987 and 1989 are also operated by Abellio Greater Anglia and primarily work the East Suffolk line, although just like the Class 153 Sprinter they can be seen on the Sudbury line and the Felixstowe line – especially if Ipswich Town Football Club are playing at home and greater capacity is needed on this line. In the past they have been drafted onto the Bury St Edmunds line to cover for an unavailable Class 170 Turbostar.

ONE replaced their Class 150 Sprinters with Class 156 Sprinters and swapped their units with Central Trains. They received nine Class 156 Sprinters – 156402, 156407, 156409, 156412, 156416–156419 and 156422. These units can also be seen at Norwich working services to Great Yarmouth, Lowestoft and Sheringham.

Class 170 Turbostar diesel multiple units

These two- and three-carriage 100-mph units were built in 1999 and 2002 and are operated by Abellio Greater Anglia. They can be seen on the Bury St Edmunds line on both Ipswich to Cambridge and Peterborough services, though they also operate on the East Suffolk line and, like the Class 156 Sprinter, on the Felixstowe line if a capacity boost is required.

Class 170 Turbostar diesel multiple unit No. 170208 sits stabled round the back of Norwich station. This unit encountered issues earlier in the day and required attention.

The first batch of eight three-carriage Turbostars (170201–170208) were originally built to work Norwich–London Liverpool Street services alongside the Class 86 loco-hauled services until they were replaced with more loco-hauled sets and found themselves working services such as Lowestoft/Peterborough–London Liverpool Street, which ran until 2010 due to these long services overcrowding a three-carriage unit.

The second batch of Class 170 Turbostars (170270–170273) have also moved over towards Ipswich as they have become too small to operate the Norwich–Cambridge line they were originally built for.

Class 315 electric multiple units

These four-carriage suburban units built in York Works in 1980/81 have spent an unglamorous life working out of London Liverpool Street on services to Shenfield, Cheshunt, Chingford and Hertford East. These 75-mph units are designed for stopping and starting frequently. This is reflected by their interiors, as they have no first class seating and no facilities such as toilets on-board.

When privatisation was complete the Class 315s were split between two operators – First Great Western and West Anglia Great Northern (WAGN) – until the franchise merger in 2004 in which they all became operated by ONE. Soon all the varying liveries they had worn over the years were replaced by the house colour of blue, with a rainbow stripe on each end of the carriage. Not only did the Class 315s receive a new paint scheme, they were also refurbished internally. This work continued as the operator changed hands; Abellio Greater Anglia continued to refurbish these units, changing the blue from the National Express period to the familiar white and red that became synonymous with them while also installing passenger information screens and an area for cycles and wheelchairs.

The days appeared to be numbered for the Class 315s on the Great Eastern Main Line as the operator for the Shenfield–London Liverpool Street section changed hands in 2015, with this line becoming part of the new Crossrail service that would eventually run to Reading via London Liverpool Street and London Paddington and allow a connection from Essex and the east end of London to the west side of London and onwards to Berkshire. As a result, new trains were introduced by Bombardier in the form of the Class 345 Aventra EMUs, which have a larger capacity to hold more passengers – 1,500 on a 345 opposed to 318 on a 315. They also have more facilities on-board such as free WiFi and real time location.

London Overground, who took over the Class 315 operations from London Liverpool Street to Chingford and Cheshunt over the Lea Valley lines in 2015, have also announced that they plan to replace their fleet of Class 315s with Bombardier Class 710 Aventra EMUs.

Class 315 electric multiple unit No. 315846 sits at Shenfield awaiting an all station stop Metro service to London Liverpool Street.

Class 321 electric multiple units

A unit that has spent a lot of its life on the Great Eastern Main Line, going as far back as Network SouthEast days, are the 100-mph Class 321 four-carriage EMUs built in York between 1988 and 1991 by British Rail Engineering Limited (BREL).

The Class 321 consists of three different subclasses but only the /3s and /4s have worked on the Great Eastern Main Line providing services to Southend Victoria, Clacton-on-Sea, Walton-on-the-Naze, Colchester Town, Harwich and Ipswich.

They were built to replace some of the older first-generation EMUs that were already working on the Great Eastern Main Line, such as classes 305, 308 and 309. These new units were introduced to the area in the very attractive Network SouthEast livery, providing more colour to these areas.

Again, privatisation meant that these units were divided between operators as they worked not only the Great Eastern Main Line, but also the West Coast Main Line from London Euston to places such as Rugby, Northampton and Birmingham New Street. Seventy-seven units were allocated to First Great Eastern to work services to Southend Victoria, Clacton-on-Sea, Walton-on-the-Naze, Colchester Town, Harwich and Ipswich. These later passed over to ONE, unusually though only one 321 ever received the house colours of ONE with the rest remaining in their previous liveries. When ONE changed their name to National Express East Anglia in 2008, a new livery for their units and stations followed. Shortly afterwards the Class 321s were starting to receive a new livery of grey and white when it was announced that National Express East Anglia were to lose their franchise as a result of them giving back the East Coast Main Line franchise (National Express East Coast). The livery changed from grey and white to just plain white and was referred to as polar bear livery.

All of the /3 and /4 321s now work on the Great Eastern Main Line as London Midland had a fleet of thirty-seven 321s, which were later replaced with Class 350 Desiro EMUs built by Siemens in Germany. Seventeen went to National Express East Anglia, where they would work on the Great Eastern Main Line and were not too difficult to notice as they were drafted into service in East Anglia still wearing the livery of their predecessor – bright green in a sea of grey and white. Thirteen were also given to First Capital Connect with ten of these also transferred to Abellio Greater Anglia.

In 2013, 321448 was unveiled in an unusual livery to the unsuspecting public. As this was a demonstrator unit that had been unveiled by Eversholt, who owned the Class 321s and lease them to Abellio Greater Anglia, this unit allowed passengers to experience a new travelling experience that would eventually start to be rolled out on the rest of the Class 321 fleet. Some upgrades included:

- New air-conditioning and heating systems throughout.
- On-board WiFi.
- Power sockets to allow passengers to charge laptops and phones.
- New interior surfaces.
- A new disabled toilet to allow it to pass DDR regulations.

At the time of writing these units are still being refurbished with the /3s being refurbished first.

Class 321 electric multiple unit No. 321315 sits at Colchester with a service for Walton-On-The-Naze.

Class 360 Desiro electric multiple units

A German invasion occurred on the Great Eastern Main Line in 2003 when First Great Eastern ordered twenty-one brand new Class 360 Desiros to replace the elderly Class 321s that were still running. These units are not too dissimilar to the Class 321s that were already working on the Great Eastern Main Line but are fourteen years older.

Twenty-one (360101–360121) four-carriage Class 360 Desiros were built for the Great Eastern Main Line and despite them fitting into their new services very well they stuck out on the Great Eastern Main Line like a sore thumb in their new First Great Eastern Barbie livery among the Anglia turquoise and First Great Eastern grey, blue and green. They were originally to be built with a gangway door connection like the rest of the Desiro EMU fleet around the country, but due to driver vision restriction this was dropped.

The livery wasn't the only difference with these units; they also had a different type of coupler, whereas the 321s used a tightlock coupling that allowed it couple to other units such as Class 317s and Class 323s. The Class 360s had a Dellner coupling that meant they were only able to couple with other Class 360 Desiros since they were incompatible with other units. This caused issues should they have failed and needed assistance being dragged.

Class 321s and Class 360s share one similarity, which is that only one of each class member received the company's livery before it was changed. Whereas with the Class 321s only 321446 received ONE livery before becoming National Express East

Anglia, 360115 was the only Desiro to receive National Express East Anglia livery before the franchise was turned over to Abellio Greater Anglia. Now they all wear a base livery of blue with a white stripe through the middle depicting the company's logo – with them due to be replaced in 2019, they won't be receiving a new livery before then.

Class 360 Desiro electric multiple unit No. 360119 sits at Ipswich in the cold and wet with a service recently arrived from London Liverpool Street.

Services on the GEML

After privatisation there were three operators working in and out of London Liverpool Street. Anglia Railways operated fast inter-city services to/from Norwich with occasional boat trains to/from Harwich International. First Great Eastern operated fast and semi-fast services to/from Braintree, Clacton-On-Sea, Colchester Town, Ipswich, Harwich Town, Southend Victoria and Walton-on-the-Naze. They also ran services on the Sudbury–Marks Tey and Wickford–Southminster branches as well as the metro service to/from Shenfield to London Liverpool Street. West Anglia Great Northern (WAGN) who slow and semi-fast services to/from Chingford, Cheshunt, Enfield Town, Hertford East and Stansted Express services to/from Stansted Airport.

It was decided in 2002 that it would be better, following a franchise restructuring, that only one operator should work all these services out of London Liverpool Street and across east and west Anglia. In 2003 it was announced that National Express had won the franchise after being shortlisted with Arriva and GB Railways, who later that year were later bought out by First group. In April 2004 National Express took over the entire operations for east and west Anglia introducing an attractive blue livery with rainbow stripes replacing a sea of turquoise, white and purple of the previous franchise holders.

Branch Lines on the GEML

Multiple branch lines connect onto the Great Eastern Main Line to/from Suffolk and Essex, from the north to the south the branch lines are:

Ipswich–Ely line (aka The Bury line)

Just north of Stowmarket is the Ipswich–Ely line, which can be accessed from Haughley junction and allows passengers to travel to Cambridge and Peterborough with further connections for the Midlands and the North via Bury St Edmunds, its station are as follows:

- Ipswich
- Stowmarket
- Bury St Edmunds
- Ely
- March
- Manea
- Whittlesea
- Peterborough

- Ipswich
- Needham Market
- Stowmarket
- Elmswell
- Thurston
- Bury St Edmunds
- Kennett
- Newmarket
- Dullingham
- Cambridge

The main purpose of the Ely–Ipswich line is to transport commuters from the busy town of Ipswich to the cities of Cambridge, Ely and Peterborough, with the two services seen above both operated by Abellio Greater Anglia. The two services are a twice-hourly Ipswich–Peterborough service and an hourly Ipswich–Cambridge service. Both are operated using Class 170 Turbostars, though Class 156 Sprinters can also be seen operating the line deputising for an unavailable Class 170 Turbostar.

This line has also played the important role as a relief line in the past if there have been issues on the Great Eastern Main Line or the Breckland line. Passengers have been able to use the Ely–Ipswich line to change at Stowmarket to reach Norwich, Ely or Cambridge. Despite it adding more time to journeys it ensures that passengers are still able to reach their destinations without having the need for a rail replacement bus or waiting for services to return to normal again.

Felixstowe line

This 12-mile single-track branch line can be accessed from Ipswich and forms part of the East Suffolk lines that also run on a different line to Lowestoft. This line allows passengers to travel to the seaside resort of Felixstowe, which could be mistaken as a freight-only line for the amount of freight trains that pass up and down the line. Up to thirty-three freight trains run on this line between Ipswich and Felixstowe on a weekday. Despite the high level of freight that appears on this branch line Abellio Greater Anglia are still able to provide an hourly service utilising a Class 153 Sprinter, although sometimes certain occasions could mean that a Class 156 Sprinter or Class 170 Turbostar is used instead. The stations on the Felixstowe line are as follows:

- Ipswich
- Westerfield
- Derby Road
- Trimley
- Felixstowe

The Mayflower line

From Manningtree passengers can travel on an 11-mile branch line to Harwich. Most of the services on this line serve either Harwich International or Harwich town from Manningtree, although services to/from Colchester and London Liverpool Street also serve this line during certain parts of the day. As the line is electrified the services on this line are served by Class 321s and Class 360 Desiros. DMUs serve this line as there is an early morning service from Harwich to Cambridge and a late evening to Harwich International from Cambridge that is usually operated by a Class 170 Turbostar. This line has six stations:

- Manningtree
- Mistley
- Wrabness
- Harwich International
- Dovercourt
- Harwich Town

This line has many attractions with passengers able to alight at Wrabness for footpaths that allow closer looks across this line. It runs on the edge of the RSPB Stour Estuary Reserve, so passengers don't even need to alight to see some the attractions of this line if their interest involves birds. Harwich International is the main port for both freight and passenger ships as holiday makers can reach the Hook of Holland from Harwich International by ferry. With container ships also loading and unloading at Harwich it means that there is a freight train not too far behind with GBRF serving this port from places such as Hams Hall in Birmingham.

This line was named the Mayflower line after Christopher Jones, who was born in Harwich in 1570 and was the captain of a pilgrim ship called the *Mayflower* that transported English pilgrims from Plymouth, Devon to America in 1620.

The Sunshine Coast line

From Colchester, passengers don't need to travel far to get to the coast as they can travel to either Clacton-on-Sea or Walton-on-the-Naze. Both lines are 18 miles long and both can be picked up from Colchester. On the return journeys the trains differ as services from Clacton-on-Sea operate services back to London Liverpool Street and services from Walton-on-the-Naze operate only as far as Colchester. Passengers must change at Thorpe-le-Soken to travel to Walton-on-the-Naze – the stations/services are as follows:

- Colchester
- Wivenhoe
- Thorpe-le-Soken
- Clacton-on-Sea

- Colchester
- Colchester Town
- Hythe
- Wivenhoe
- Alresford
- Great Bentley
- Weeley
- Thorpe-le-Soken
- Kirby Cross
- Frinton-on-Sea
- Walton-on-the-Naze

Again, these services are operated by Class 321 and Class 360 EMUs, usually in four-, eight- and twelve-carriage formations as both lines are electrified. These lines were electrified during the 1950s and in the 1960s they were originally operated by Class 309 EMUs, which were designed and built especially for these lines.

Between 2006 and 2009 these lines were improved as part of a £100 million upgrade. The signalling equipment was in desperate need of being upgraded and therefore every weekend during this period the signals, which were an old style of searchlight signal, were replaced with over 170 LED signals. Eight level crossings were also upgraded. The control for these lines were also passed over to a new modernised signal box at Colchester.

The Gainsborough line

The 11-mile branch line to Sudbury, Suffolk, also known as the Gainsborough line, connects to the Great Eastern Main Line from Marks Tey and is served by an hourly service, usually with a Class 153 Sprinter DMU although a Class 156 Sprinter DMU can be seen operating the line when extra capacity is needed. This line consists of four stations:

- Marks Tey
- Chappel & Wakes Colne
- Bures
- Sudbury

Before reaching the first station of Chappel & Wakes Colne, passengers travel over the eye-catching Chappel viaduct, which has thirty-two arches and a span of 30 feet that sit at a height of 75 feet. This attractive structure built in 1847 and finished in 1849 needed seven million bricks and still attracts travellers to this day looking to soak in the brilliance of this engineering achievement as well as the views that can be seen from the top from the train.

At Chappel & Wakes Colne passengers can also alight for the East Anglian Railway Museum, which opened in 1986 and houses a variety of different trains as well as driver experience days, a miniature railway and a goods and restoration shed to explore. One of the trains on display at the EARM is a Class 306 EMU, which is owned by the National Railway Museum (NRM) and has been loaned to the EARM. These units are no stranger to the Great Eastern Main Line as they were used on Shenfield–London Liverpool Street stopping services before they were replaced with the current Class 315s.

The reason this line is named the Gainsborough line is because of Thomas Gainsborough, a famous portrait painter born in Sudbury who later became the favourite painter of George III and was a founding member of the Royal Academy in London.

Braintree branch line

This 6-mile branch line can be found at Witham and allows passengers to travel to Braintree, Essex. This line is electrified and has an hourly service operating on it with services to and from London Liverpool Street. Either a Class 321 EMU or Class 360 will operate the services to and from London Liverpool Street, although it isn't unusual to find a Class 317 operating these services from time to time especially on weekend.

The Braintree branch altogether has five stations, which are as follows:

- Witham
- White Notley
- Cressing
- Braintree Freeport
- Braintree

This line is very popular with shoppers because of the large shopping mall at Braintree Freeport. The station there opened in 1999 and no doubt increased passenger numbers.

The Southend and Crouch Valley lines

At Shenfield one line diverges to the left heading towards Chelmsford and on the right-hand side of the station another line joins the Great Eastern Main Line. These lines make up the Southend line, which is a 21-mile electrified line that allows passengers to travel to the coastal city of Southend-on-Sea. There are nine stations altogether that make up the Southend line:

- Shenfield
- Billericay

- Wickford
- Rayleigh
- Hockley
- Rochford
- Southend Airport
- Prittlewell
- Southend Victoria

This line is double track throughout and sees a train departing for London Liverpool Street every twenty minutes every day. Only Class 321 EMUs operate the London Liverpool Street-Southend services.

At Wickford another branch line. This is the Crouch Valley line, which is sixteen miles long and allows passengers to travel to Southminster. The name is derived from the river Crouch, which can be seen and walked along between North Fambridge and Althorne. Like the Southend line, it is electrified. It is only operated by Class 321 EMUs, and the stations are:

- Wickford
- Battlesbridge
- South Woodham Ferrers
- North Fambridge
- Althorne
- Burnham-on-Crouch
- Southminster

The services typically operate between Southminster and Wickford all day with services leaving Wickford every forty minutes, though during the morning peak and in the evening some services can run to London Liverpool Street or Shenfield.

All the images taken in this book on the Great Eastern Main Line are my own and were taken within the safety rules and regulations of the railways. Remember the railways are a dangerous place and can kill if mistreated.

The time period for these images is 2016–2019, when Abellio Greater Anglia had just been awarded a nine-year franchise to run in East Anglia.

All Norwich services to and from the capital are operated by loco-hauled sets with Class 90s at the helm. For a short period of time they meet at London Liverpool Street – Nos 90011 and 90010 meet at London with services for Norwich.

A wide variety of EMUs can be seen at London Liverpool Street. Despite three Class 379 Electrostars dominating, a Class 317 and Class 321 can also be seen and all are serving various destinations across East and West Anglia.

Two common units that can be seen on the Great Eastern Main Line are Class 360 Desiros and Class 321s. No. 360118 awaits departure for the hourly service for Ipswich while No. 321447 awaits departure for Southend Victoria, which sees a frequent service throughout the day.

Introduced in 2009 by National Express East Anglia to provide a faster service towards Cambridge and Stansted Airport, the Class 379 Electrostar operates from London to Stansted Airport every 15 minutes to provide a fast and frequent service.

Abellio Greater Anglia Class 321 EMU No. 321440 sits at London Liverpool Street stabled between duties.

An EMU that has been working out of London Liverpool Street since Network SouthEast days is the Class 317. These units were built between the early to mid-1980s and have worked many services from London Liverpool Street towards destinations such as Cambridge, Hertford East and Stansted Airport. Here Class 317 No. 317345 awaits departure.

It isn't unusual to see a Class 357 Electrostar at London Liverpool Street. These are operated by C2C to destinations such as Grays, Shoeburyness and Southend. They look very similar to the Class 170 Turbostar despite being completely different units. Class 357 Electrostar No. 357210 sits at London Liverpool Street with a service for Shoeburyness with TfL Rail Class 315 No. 315855 on a Metro service for Shenfield.

Not technically on the Great Eastern Main Line but providing a great vantage point of trains arriving into and departing London Liverpool Street is Bethnal Green station, located a mile outside the London terminus. TfL Class 345 Aventra No. 345008 starts the descent into London Liverpool Street alongside Abellio Greater Anglia Class 360 Desiro No. 360116 while Abellio Greater Anglia Class 82 DVT No. 82143 and London Overground Class 317 No. 317892 head towards Norwich and Enfield Town.

Abellio Greater Anglia Class 317 No. 317661 passes through Bethnal Green with a service for Cambridge. This will turn off the Great Eastern Main Line and head down the West Anglia Main Line (WAML) via Tottenham Hale and Cheshunt.

C2C Class 357 Electrostar No. 357017 departs from London Liverpool Street with a driver training run originating from Barking and terminating at Seven Kings.

Abellio Greater Anglia Class 321 No. 321319 heads up the bank heading towards Orient Way carriage sidings. These units will stable here for the duration of the day and will return back into London Liverpool Street in preparation for the evening peak.

Coming off the Great Eastern Main Line for arrival into Bethnal Green is London Overground Class 315 EMU No. 315814 with a service for Chingford. London Overground inherited a fleet of seventeen Class 315s from Abellio Greater Anglia in 2015, as well as ownership of the lines from London Liverpool Street to Chingford, Enfield Town and Cheshunt via Seven Sisters.

TfL Rail Class 345 Aventra No. 345017 heads towards its first stop of Stratford. These new units make light work of the ascent out of London compared to the steam engines of the 1950s, which would have required considerable effort to reach the top – even more so in wet weather conditions.

TfL Rail Class 315 EMU No. 315854 passes through Bethnal Green with a Metro service for Shenfield.

Abellio Greater Anglia Class 360 Desiro No. 360121 passes Bethnal Green with a service for Colchester Town. This is an hourly service that runs Monday–Saturday, calling at eight stations and arriving into the Essex town in just over an hour.

4 miles north of London Liverpool Street is Stratford station, which sees both passenger and freight services – the latter having to be fitted between the passenger services. Freightliner Class 86 No. 86605, leading No. 86612, passes through Platform 10a. This platform also acts as a passing loop as this service for Felixstowe will be held until a path is available to join the Great Eastern Main Line.

A common freight train seen on the southern part of the Great Eastern Main Line is a sand train that runs between Acton in West London to Chelmsford in Essex. This freight train is operated by DB and is hauled by either a Class 59 or 66 diesel locomotive depending on availability. DB Class 66 diesel locomotive No. 66002 passes through Stratford heading towards Acton via the North London Line.

Abellio Greater Anglia services from Norwich provide an hourly service to London Liverpool Street at Stratford. Class 90 No. 90014 arrives into Stratford with a service for London Liverpool Street. This Class 90 was named *Norfolk and Norwich Festival* in 2006.

Class 321 EMUs, all operated by Abellio Greater Anglia, provide a frequent service to destinations such as Braintree, Colchester, Ipswich, Southend, or, as seen by Class 321 EMU No. 321435, services towards Clacton-on-Sea.

Class 357 Electrostars can also be seen at Stratford. On this day Class 357 Electrostar EMU No. 357016 was being used for driver training diagrams between Stratford and London Liverpool Street.

A new EMU to arrive onto the Great Eastern Main Line is the Class 345 Aventra built by Bombardier in Derby. These units are replacing Class 315 EMUs on services between London Liverpool Street and Shenfield, which will get extended once Crossrail is opened towards West London and Reading in Berkshire.

Class 315 EMUs provide a very frequent service between Shenfield and London Liverpool Street, with a set arriving every ten minutes heading in both directions. Class 315 EMU No. 315853 leads a service into Stratford bound for the capital.

Also 4 miles north of London is Maryland station, one of many that make up Metro services between Shenfield and London Liverpool Street. TfL Class 315s Nos 315829 and 315830 meet at Maryland (just), with services for Shenfield and London Liverpool Street.

On 11 February 2019 a block on the fast line heading into London between Manor Park and Maryland meant all fast services had to share the slow lines with the Metro services. Abellio Greater Anglia Class 360 Desiro No. 360106 passes through Maryland with a service for London Liverpool Street.

TfL Rail Class 345 Aventra No. 345014 arrives into Maryland with a service for London Liverpool Street.

Abellio Greater Anglia Class 321 No. 321422 passes Maryland with a service for Clacton-on-Sea.

Abellio Greater Anglia Class 82 DVT 82105 slowly builds up speed from its booked station stop at Stratford with a service for Norwich.

TfL Rail Class 315 EMU No. 315818 arrives into Maryland with a service for Shenfield.

Freightliner Class 66 No. 66534 joins the Great Eastern Main Line with a liner train towards Felixstowe.

5 miles from London is Forest Gate station. Here TfL Rail Class 345 Aventras Nos 345017 and 345008 arrive with services for London Liverpool Street and Shenfield.

Abellio Greater Anglia Class 321 No. 321445 passes through Forest Gate with a service for London Liverpool Street.

Abellio Greater Anglia Class 90 No. 90004 *City of Chelmsford* passes through the slow line at Forest Gate with a service for London Liverpool Street. The slow lines are 20 mph slower than the fast line, thus causing a slight delay with the faster services into London.

Freightliner Class 66 locomotive No. 66565 passes Forest Gate with a freight train from Felixstowe to Ditton Freightliner Terminal, located in Widnes, Cheshire. This freight was stuck on the fast lines at Manor Park, resulting in other services taking the slow lines.

Abellio Greater Anglia Class 360 Desiro No. 360106 passes through Forest Gate with a service for Clacton-on-Sea.

Abellio Greater Anglia Class 360 Desiro No. 360107 passes through Forest Gate heading towards London Liverpool Street. Note the destination, which despite being programmed into the Desiro and visiting once on a test run, has never done a passenger service.

Abellio Greater Anglia Class 82 DVT No. 82121 powers through the station with a service for Norwich.

TfL Rail Class 315 EMU No. 315820 arrives into Forest Gate with a service for London Liverpool Street.

A mile further sits Manor Park station. TfL Rail Class 315 EMU No. 315826 arrives into the station with a service for Shenfield.

Passengers are protected from the trains on the fast lines by means of a fence that goes right down the middle of the platform. Abellio Greater Anglia Class 360 Desiro No. 360104 passes through with a service for London Liverpool Street.

Also seen on a driver training run, having originated from Ilford EMU depot, was C2C Class 357 Electrostar No. 357323, passing through Manor Park. The unit was built as No. 357223 but was modified with its 3+2 seating replaced with 2+2 seating and more standing areas available for passengers. As a result this was re-classed as a high-density unit.

Double-headed freight trains on the Great Eastern Main Line aren't an unusual sight, often because the first loco failed at some point on the journey and the second loco was used to rescue it. This isn't the case here as Freightliner Class 66s Nos 66552 and 66545 head through Manor Park with a liner from Wentloog in Cardiff to Felixstowe North freight terminal.

Parked in many different sidings across the UK, different track maintenance trains can be seen stabled. These are usually used during the night when there are no trains left running on the network. Painted in a very striking and noticeable yellow they are easily visible, as seen here as DR73116 passes heading towards Romford.

Abellio Greater Anglia Class 82 DVT No. 82139 passes Manor Park with a service for Norwich.

Abellio Greater Anglia Class 360 Desiro No. 360110 passes Manor Park with a service for Clacton-on-Sea.

TfL Rail Class 315 EMU No. 315830 arrives into Forest Gate with a service for London Liverpool Street.

7 miles from London Liverpool Street is Ilford. TfL Rail Class 345 Aventra No. 345017 arrives into the station with a service for London Liverpool Street.

Abellio Greater Anglia Class 321 No. 321410 passes Ilford with a service for London Liverpool Street, still wearing its former colours of First Capital Connect it was drafted over to Abellio Greater Anglia to help ease overcrowding on the Great Eastern Main Line during peak periods.

Freightliner Class 66 No. 66571 passes through Ilford with a liner train from Felixstowe North to Trafford Park in Manchester.

8 miles away from London Liverpool Street is Seven Kings station. TfL Rail Class 315 EMU No. 315852 arrives into the station with a service for London Liverpool Street.

9 miles away from London Liverpool Street sits Goodmayes station. TfL Rail Class 315 EMU No. 315829 arrives into the station with a service for London Liverpool Street. The EMU is named *London Borough of Havering Celebrating 40 years*.

Abellio Greater Anglia Class 321 EMU No. 321320 passes Goodmayes with a service for London Liverpool Street.

Abellio Greater Anglia Class 90 No. 90003 heads through Goodmayes with a service from Norwich towards London Liverpool Street. A Class 90 can complete these diagrams in roughly two hours.

With a brief wave from the driver, Abellio Greater Anglia Class 360 Desiro No. 360115 passes Goodmayes with a service for London Liverpool Street.

Also the same distance as Goodmayes is Chadwell Heath station. Abellio Greater Anglia Class 321 EMU No. 321422 powers through the station. This 321 originally belonged to Silverlink before transferring to previous operator National Express East Anglia and repainted into what was known as Polar Bear livery.

TfL Rail Class 315 EMU No. 315830 arrives into Chadwell Heath with a service for London Liverpool Street.

12 miles from London Liverpool Street is Romford station, which is served by three different operators. One of these is TfL, with Class 345 Aventra No. 345014 arriving into the station with a service for London Liverpool Street.

Abellio Greater Anglia Class 82 DVT No. 82114 passes through the station with a service for Norwich.

The second operator that serves Romford is London Overground, which provides a half-hourly service on the 3-mile branch line to Upminster. This branch line originally run by Abellio Greater Anglia changed hands in 2015 with the services on the West Anglia Main Line towards Chingford and Cheshunt.

The third operator that serves Romford is Abellio Greater Anglia, who provide a half-hourly service towards London Liverpool Street and an hourly service towards Southend Victoria and Colchester Town. Abellio Greater Anglia Class 321 EMU No. 321349 passes through Romford with a service for Braintree.

Abellio Greater Anglia Class 360 Desiro No. 360113 passes Romford with a service for London Liverpool Street.

13 miles from London Liverpool Street is Gidea Park station, where a lot of TfL units are stored in a yard just outside the station when not required. In the late afternoon sunshine Abellio Greater Anglia Class 321 EMU No. 321302 passes through the station with a service for London Liverpool Street.

14 miles away is Harold Wood station which, as seen in this image, is in the process of being extended. TfL Rail Class 315 EMU No. 315827 arrives with a service for London Liverpool Street.

Abellio Greater Anglia Class 360 Desiro No. 360102 passes through the station with a service for London Liverpool Street.

Abellio Greater Anglia Class 321 EMU No. 321301 passes through Harold Wood with a service for London Liverpool Street. A unit built thirty years ago, they are still providing sterling service on the Great Eastern Main Line.

Located at the top of a bank, which was notoriously difficult for steam engines in the past, is Brentwood. Today's freight trains slowly climb this bank with no issues. Freightliner Class 66 No. 66559 heads through Brentwood and down the bank towards the North London line with a freight train for Lawley Street Freightliner terminal in Birmingham.

TfL Rail Class 345 Aventra No. 345005 arrives into Brentwood with a service for London Liverpool Street.

Living on borrowed time is TfL Rail Class 315 EMU No. 315818 as it sits with a service for London Liverpool Street.

Abellio Greater Anglia Class 321 EMU No. 321422 leads a classmate through the station with a service for London Liverpool Street.

20 miles away from London Liverpool Street and at the end of the Metro section is Shenfield station, where the lines for Southend Victoria and Southminster diverge from the Great Eastern Main Line. Abellio Greater Anglia Class 90 No. 90013 passes through the station with a service for London Liverpool Street. These services used to stop at this station before it was removed from the timetable in 2010.

An unusual and very rare rescue occurred on the Great Eastern Main Line on 28 October 2017 when a freight train from Hams Hall in Birmingham to Felixstowe slid to a halt on Brentwood bank. The leading locomotive, which was GBRF Class 66 No. 66759, was unable to pull the heavy freight train up the bank as the locomotive behind it, No. 66745, had run low on fuel and therefore was dead in train. Running late and blocking the fast line the railhead treatment train (RHTT), formed of a pair of DRS Class 57/3s – Nos 57303 and 57306, was sent to assist the train up the bank and towards Colchester. Here the convoy passes through Shenfield bound for Colchester before another loco took the train onwards to Felixstowe.

A Great Eastern Main Line relic, which spent many years sat at Shenfield, is this brake van. Its number is DB993733 and it has been sitting in that siding for a number of years – to this day it remains in the siding next to Platform 1 at Shenfield with its future unknown. Moving it to the nearby Epping Ongar Railway was once attempted, but it sadly never made it there.

Abellio Greater Anglia Class 360 Desiro No. 360117 arrives into Shenfield with a service for Colchester Town. Shenfield sees a half-hourly service to Southend Victoria and an hourly service to Braintree, Clacton-on-Sea, Colchester and Ipswich.

Abellio Greater Anglia Class 321 EMU No. 321425 departs on the rear of a service for London Liverpool Street. This service started from Southend Victoria and will stop only at Stratford on its way towards the capital.

Ready to start another Metro service towards London Liverpool Street is TfL Rail Class 315 EMU No. 315855. This will stop at all stations and will take just over forty minutes to cover this 20-mile section.

When engineering works occur on the Great Eastern Main Line the loco-hauled sets may terminate further north from London Liverpool Street than usual before turning back. On 24 November 2018, engineering works on the fast line meant that only the slow line was open and as a result these sets terminated at Shenfield. No. 90011 sits at Shenfield awaiting departure for Norwich, sat next to it is No. 360120 with an Ipswich service.

23 miles from London Liverpool Street is Ingatestone, a small village based in Essex. There are only two signal boxes left on the Great Eastern Main Line, one based here and the other at Stowmarket. Since 1996 the box only controls the level crossing next to it.

Abellio Greater Anglia Class 360 Desiro No. 360118 passes through Ingatestone with a service for Colchester Town.

A pair of Freightliner Class 86 electric locomotives pass through Ingatestone with a train from Coatbridge to Felixstowe. These locomotives always work in pairs on the Great Eastern Main Line and as a result it is possible to see the two different variations of livery as No. 86622 is wearing the newer Powerhaul livery and No. 86613 is still wearing the older Freightliner green livery.

Two trains an hour stop at Ingatestone for London Liverpool Street, one starting from Clacton-on-Sea and the other from Braintree. A pair of Class 321 EMUs led by No. 321347 arrive into Ingatestone with a service from Braintree.

On 17 November 2018 the Great Eastern Main Line was closed again for engineering works while the line was being upgraded in preparation for Crossrail. Therefore, the loco-hauled sets from Norwich were only able to run as far as Ingatestone. In the afternoon sunshine No. 90008 rests before heading back to Norwich.

On weekends it is common to see a pair of Class 317 EMUs on the Great Eastern Main Line providing a service from London Liverpool Street to Braintree; a change of scenery for Class 317 EMU No. 317653 as it passes Ingatestone many miles away from its usual stamping ground on the West Anglia Main Line.

Abellio Greater Anglia Class 360 Desiro No. 360106 passes Ingatestone with a service for London Liverpool Street.

The half-hourly loco hauled sets don't stop at Ingatestone, as seen here as Abellio Greater Anglia Class 82 DVT No. 82114 passes through the station with a service for Norwich.

29 miles away from London Liverpool Street is Chelmsford in Essex. This station sees a frequent number of services heading to London from destinations such as Norwich, Ipswich and Colchester. A majority of these services are operated by Class 321 EMUs, such as No. 321353 arriving into Chelmsford with a service for London Liverpool Street.

Abellio Greater Anglia Class 90 No. 90005 arrives into Chelmsford with a service for London Liverpool Street.

One of the many liners that pass-through Chelmsford operated by Freightliner passes. Class 66 No. 66547, not long in to its journey from Felixstowe, heads through the station heading towards Crewe.

Only half of the loco-hauled sets stop at Chelmsford. The XX.00 service from London Liverpool Street runs non-stop to Colchester. No. 82121 passes through Chelmsford with a service for Norwich.

Abellio Greater Anglia Class 90 No. 90002 departs Chelmsford with a service for Norwich. The next stop for this service will be Colchester.

Abellio Greater Anglia Class 360 Desiros Nos 360108 and 360106 arrive into Chelmsford with a service for Colchester Town.

Wearing the new Abellio Greater Anglia livery after being refurbished in the Renatus project is No. 321319, which arrives into Chelmsford with a service for Braintree.

Over fifty years old and hardly showing their age, Freightliner Class 86 Nos 86612 and 86609 pass through the quiet station of Hatfield Peveral with another working from Coatbridge to Felixstowe.

The sleepy station of Hatfield Peveral is 35 miles away from London Liverpool Street and is only served by an hourly service to Ipswich and London Liverpool Street. Abellio Greater Anglia Class 321 EMU No. 321304, looking very smart in its new Renatus livery, passes through the station with a service for Clacton-on-Sea.

Freightliner Class 66 No. 66566 passes through Hatfield Peveral with a freight train from Freightliner heading towards Wembley Yard in London.

Like many of the stations on the Great Eastern Main Line, the loco-hauled 90 sets do not serve this station as it flies through with a London Liverpool Street service.

Abellio Greater Anglia Class 360 Desiro No. 360114 arrives into Hatfield Peveral with one of the hourly services for London Liverpool Street.

Abellio Greater Anglia Class 360 Desiro No. 360103 flies through Hatfield Peveral with a Colchester Town service.

A different pair of Abellio Greater Anglia Class 317 EMUs venture onto the Great Eastern Main Line as No. 317666 passes with a Braintree service.

GBRF Class 66 No. 66771 passes through Witham station with a freight train from Felixstowe to Hams Hall. Usually this train goes via Ely and Peterborough, but due to this line being closed for engineering works it was diverted via the North London line.

38 miles from London Liverpool Street is Witham station, which sees a regular service to London Liverpool Street with four services an hour. One of these services isn't from Norwich; passengers travelling on these sets from Norwich would need to change at Colchester. No. 90014 powers through Witham with a service for London Liverpool Street.

Freightliner Class 66 No. 66508 passes through Witham with a freight train from Felixstowe North heading towards Wembley Yard in London. On a clear day the visibility from the north is so good that trains approaching can be seen from quite a distance away.

Abellio Greater Anglia Class 321 EMU No. 321338 sits at Witham with a service for Harwich International. After Witham this service will make four more station stops before arriving into the Essex port around fifty minutes later. There is also an hourly service to Clacton-on-Sea, Colchester and Ipswich from Witham.

Before 2010 it was common to see a Class 170 Turbostar south of Colchester on the Great Eastern Main Line as the line's predecessors National Express East Anglia used to run a service from Peterborough and Lowestoft to London Liverpool Street. These services were scrapped due to overcrowding as a result of the Turbostar being too small and there being too many station stops. They found a new lease of life working the Norwich–Cambridge line, aka The Breckland line. Here an Abellio Greater Anglia Class 170 Turbostar passes through Witham with an ECS movement from Ilford depot to Norwich Crown Point depot, after visiting the depot to use the wheel lathe.

Abellio Greater Anglia Class 321 EMU No. 321308 arrives into Witham with a service for London Liverpool Street.

Another pair of Freightliner 86s, Nos 86628 and 86614, head through Witham with a freight train bound for Felixstowe. Class 86s were a common sight on the Great Eastern Main Line as they were used on the Norwich–London Liverpool Street services before being replaced by Class 90s in 2004.

The 6-mile branch line to Braintree diverges to the left at Witham with an extremely tight left-hand curve. Abellio Greater Anglia Class 317 EMU No. 317663 awaits departure with a service for London Liverpool Street. Platform 4, like Platform 1 at Witham, has alternative uses as they can both be used as passing loops by freight trains on the Great Eastern Main Line to allow faster running trains to overtake.

Providing one of the hourly services to Colchester Town is former First Capital Connect now Abellio Greater Anglia Class 321 EMU No. 321408. These units have been refreshed with the Abellio Greater Anglia colours inside, but have yet to visit the paint shop for the exterior.

42 miles from London Liverpool Street sits the village of Kelvedon. Much like Hatfield Peveral it sees a small service as it has an hourly service to Colchester and Ipswich and two trains an hour to London Liverpool Street. The loco-hauled 90 sets do not serve this station either with No. 90011 speeding through heading towards the capital.

Freightliner Class 70 diesel locomotive No. 70005 passes through Kelvedon bound for Felixstowe. These locomotives arrived in the UK in 2009 and stand out from the usual Class 66s due to their distinctive look and sound.

Abellio Greater Anglia Class 321 EMU No. 321427, still wearing the colours of its predecessor National Express East Anglia, passes through Kelvedon with a service for London Liverpool Street. Note the double amber signal to the right of the 321. This station and large parts of the Great Eastern Main Line has bi-directional signalling installed to allow trains to travel 'wrong line' should something occur on the Great Eastern Main Line.

Arriving into Kelvedon with the hourly Ipswich service is Abellio Greater Anglia Class 321 EMU No. 321355. This unit previously belonged to First Great Eastern and has spent its entire life working on the Great Eastern Main Line.

Abellio Greater Anglia Class 82 DVT No. 82133 passes through Kelvedon with a service for Norwich.

Abellio Greater Anglia Class 360 Desiro No. 360117 arrives into Kelvedon with a service for London Liverpool Street. This service originated from Ipswich and has five more station stops before reaching the capital forty-five minutes later.

46 miles from London Liverpool Street is Marks Tey station, serving a nearby village of the same name. Soaking up the late afternoon sunshine is Abellio Greater Anglia Class 321 EMU No. 321308 with a service for Ipswich. This station also sees two trains an hour to London Liverpool Street, with an hourly service for Colchester and Ipswich.

Abellio Greater Anglia Class 90 No. 90007 passes through Marks Tey with a service for London Liverpool Street.

Following shortly behind No. 90007 was Class 360 Desiro No. 360102 with another London Liverpool Street service.

The 11-mile branch line to Sudbury diverges off to the right at Marks Tey. This line sees an hourly service with both Class 153 or Class 156 Sprinter DMUs covering the diagrams. On two separate occasions both No. 156418 and No. 153322 have been seen working this line.

Freightliner Class 66 No. 66564 passes through Marks Tey with a freight train from Felixstowe to Crewe Basford Hall.

Abellio Greater Anglia Class 82 DVT No. 82105 glides through Marks Tey with a service for Norwich.

51 miles from London Liverpool Street is the large station of Colchester based in Essex. This station sees a half-hourly service between Norwich and London Liverpool Street, as well as other stations such as Clacton-on-Sea, Walton-On-The-Naze and Colchester Town. Abellio Greater Anglia Class 90 No. 90008 arrives into Colchester with a service for London Liverpool Street. This loco is named *The East Anglian* after the fast weekday service between Norwich and London Liverpool Street.

Another Class 321 EMU that has spent its entire life on the Great Eastern Main Line is No. 321316, sitting at Colchester with a service for Clacton-on-Sea. Colchester sees an hourly service for Clacton-on-Sea. Colchester Town located 2 miles away, and there is a half-hourly service for Norwich and five services for London Liverpool Street.

GBRF also run liner trains alongside Freightliner on the Great Eastern Main Line. GBRF have a large fleet of Class 66s to haul their liner trains, one being No. 66768, which has just departed from the goods loop on the other side of the station – this, too, is heading for Felixstowe.

One of the benefits of a half-hourly timetable is that the loco-hauled sets will meet at certain station such as Ipswich, Manningtree and Colchester, as seen here as Nos 90014 and 82102 meet with their services for Norwich and London Liverpool Street.

Towards the end of the day the two hourly services between Ipswich and Peterborough extend out towards Colchester, the difference being that one of these units will terminate at Colchester and run into the yard to stable for the night before being used on Ipswich–Peterborough diagrams the next day, while the other unit will run empty coaching stock (ECS) back to Norwich Crown Point. Abellio Greater Anglia Class 170 Turbostar No. 170271 will be the unit to run ECS back to Norwich Crown Point after spending the day on Ipswich–Peterborough diagrams. It is seen here terminated at Colchester.

Awaiting departure for London Liverpool Street under the early evening sky is former Great Northern Class 321 No. 321409. This unit transferred to Abellio Greater Anglia after it was replaced with a Class 387 Electrostar on the East Coast Main Line.

Still proving their worth are Class 86 Nos 86605 and 86622, heading through Colchester towards Felixstowe. These locos will be removed at Ipswich and run light engine to the yard at the station there.

Gleaming under the midday sunshine is Abellio Greater Anglia Class 360 Desiro No. 360118, awaiting departure for Ipswich. This service also stops at Manningtree en route to Ipswich.

59 miles from London Liverpool Street, situated between Colchester and Ipswich, is the town of Manningtree. From here the 11-mile branch to Harwich Town turns off to the right. Abellio Greater Anglia Class 360 Desiro No. 360113 sits at Manningtree awaiting departure for Harwich again. There is an hourly service to Harwich Town operated by either a Class 321 or Class 360.

All the loco-hauled sets from Norwich and London Liverpool Street call at Manningtree, providing a half-hourly service. No. 90015 arrives into Manningtree with a service for London Liverpool Street. In 2008 this locomotive was named *Colchester Castle*.

As night time falls, No. 82105's work isn't over yet as it calls at Manningtree with a service for Norwich.

Passing through Manningtree, Freightliner Class 66 No. 66955 heads towards Felixstowe with a freight train from Lawley Street Freightliner terminal in Birmingham. The Class 66/9 subclass differs from other subclasses as it has less fuel capacity and therefore emits lower emissions than the other 66s.

Due to the Ely–Peterborough stretch being closed on the weekend of January 26 2019, freight trains heading towards Felixstowe were diverted via the Great Eastern Main Line. One of these freight trains was operated by GBRF – Class 66 No. 66743, running from Birch Coppice in Birmingham to Felixstowe. No. 66743 wears a special Belmond Royal Scotsman livery, one of two 66s wearing this – the other being No. 66746. They were painted in this livery when the contract passed from West Coast Railway Company to GBRF and they are dedicated to this train, although when they aren't needed they can be seen working other duties.

Above and below: Just outside Manningtree is Cattawade, which is a very popular spot for train enthusiasts and provides a great vantage point for any trains that pass. Abellio Greater Anglia Class 90 No. 90010 breaks the silence as it heads over the bridge on the approach to Manningtree. Abellio Greater Anglia Class 321 EMU No. 321348 can be seen departing Manningtree passing Cattawade with a service for Ipswich.

68 miles from London Liverpool Street is Ipswich station. Based in Suffolk, this is a busy station with three services to London Liverpool Street an hour. Two of these services are operated with loco-hauled Class 90 sets, which make a half-hourly service to the capital. No. 90007 arrives into Ipswich with a service for London Liverpool Street. This Class 90 was named *Sir John Betjeman* in 2006 after the famous writer and poet.

Abellio Greater Anglia Class 170 Turbostar No. 170206 sits at Ipswich with a service for Cambridge. These units also work services to Lowestoft and Peterborough and, on rare occasions, services to Felixstowe. They run services to Harwich International and Colchester towards the end of service.

The third service to London Liverpool Street is a slower service as it stops at stations like Marks Tey, Witham and Shenfield. The 90 sets, on the other hand, do not; these services leave Ipswich at 52 minutes past the hour and cover the 68 miles to London in just over an hour.

Sprinters, both Classes 153 and 156, can be seen working services to Cambridge, Lowestoft and Peterborough, either working alongside or in place of the booked Class 170 Turbostars that are designated for the diagrams. Seen here awaiting departure is No. 156412.

Both passenger and freight trains share Ipswich station, with the freight trains sometimes being a bit of a hindrance to the passenger services. As Abellio Greater Anglia Class 90 No. 90001 arrives into Ipswich with a London Liverpool Street service, Freightliner Class 66 No. 66415 slows for a crew change with a freight train for Felixstowe. No. 66415 can be seen wearing the colours of its previous operator DRS, which it still wears to this day.

Freightliner operate a small fleet of ten Class 90 electric locomotives; these can be seen working the same diagrams as the Class 86s. The Freightliner 90s have three different liveries – Freightliner green, Powerhaul, and, as seen on No. 90048, a two-tone grey livery that it has worn since before privatisation. No. 90048 is shunting into Ipswich Yard after being removed from its freight train due to the Felixstowe line being unelectrified.

Most freight trains come from Felixstowe that head through Ipswich heading to places such as Birmingham and Crewe in the West Midlands. Freightliner Class 66 No. 66543 passes through Ipswich with an empty freight train for Crewe Basford Hall.

Every year tailhead treatment trains (RHTT) operate all over the Great Eastern Main Line, keeping the rails clean from leaf mulch that can cause damage to train wheelsets as they are unable to grip the rails when departing. Direct Rail Services (DRS) operate this contract every year in East Anglia and are always in the interest of train enthusiasts due to type of diesel locomotives that operate these diagrams. On 20 October 2018 a Class 37 diesel locomotive, No. 37038, and Class 57 diesel locomotive No. 57301 work this diagram towards Shenfield and Clacton-on-Sea.

Between Ipswich and Stowmarket lies the quiet station of Needham Market. This station doesn't have direct services to London Liverpool Street, with a change at Ipswich needed. The Ipswich–Peterborough service, which runs once every two hours, usually with Class 170 Turbostars, runs non-stop from Stowmarket to Ipswich as seen with No. 170270.

DB Class 66 No. 66030 heads through Needham Market, nearing journey's end as it heads to Barham freight terminal just outside Ipswich. This freight train originated from Mountsorrel in Leicestershire.

On a pleasant summer's afternoon Abellio Greater Anglia Class 156 Sprinter No. 156407 arrives into Needham Market with a service for Cambridge.

GBRF Class 66 No. 66747 powers through Needham Market with a freight train from Felixstowe heading towards Masborough in Rotherham. This Class 66, alongside two others (Nos 66748 and 66749), originally used to work in Europe before being transferred and converted in the UK.

Services to/from Norwich have never stopped at Needham Market. Much like the Peterborough services they run non-stop from either Diss or Stowmarket to Ipswich. Abellio Greater Anglia Class 90 No. 90013 passes with a service for London Liverpool Street.

Abellio Greater Anglia Class 82 DVT No. 82121 passes Needham Market with a service for Norwich.

80 miles from London Liverpool Street sits Stowmarket station and, like Ingatestone station, this too has a signal box that has been downgraded. Since 1985 this box has only operated the two nearby level crossings just outside the station.

Stowmarket sees a half-hourly service to London Liverpool Street from Norwich, with the XX.30 service being a fast service stopping only at Diss, Ipswich, Colchester and finally London Liverpool Street. As fellow classmate No. 90012 heads towards Norwich, No. 90011 passes through Stowmarket with a fast service for London Liverpool Street.

Abellio Greater Anglia Class 170 Turbostar No. 170207 arrives into Stowmarket with a service for Cambridge. These units can also be seen working Peterborough services, which also stop here.

Seen on 1 February 2019, Abellio Greater Anglia Class 755 FLIRT BMU is on test on the Great Eastern Main Line and builds up speed as it passes through Stowmarket. Earlier in the day it encountered an issue at Ipswich and the test runs for the rest of the day were cancelled.

Outside the station is a small yard, which is most commonly used to stable track machines and the yearly railhead treatment trains. DRS Class 57 No. 57002 and Class 37 No. 37602 sit in the yard awaiting their next turn around East Anglia while Abellio Greater Anglia Class 82 DVT No. 82127 arrives with a service for Norwich.

Covering for an unavailable Class 170 Turbostar, Abellio Greater Anglia Class 156 Sprinter No. 156407 arrives into Stowmarket with a service for Cambridge.

In extreme cases, to avoid cancelling the diagram units such as these small Class 153 Sprinters will be used. Before massive timetable changes in 2010 these units regularly worked Cambridge–Ipswich diagrams before being deemed too small due to the massive passenger growth. On this day, No. 153314 was drafted in to work Cambridge–Ipswich diagrams all day, which resulted in a very busy, packed train.

Stowmarket is very common for freight, especially if the Great Eastern Main Line is closed for engineering works south of Ipswich. A new freight chord opened outside Ipswich station in 2014, which meant that freight trains could head towards Stowmarket and Bury St Edmunds without needing to change ends in the yard. Freightliner Class 66 No. 66562 sits at Stowmarket after a crew change with a freight train bound for Daventry in Northamptonshire.

GBRF Class 66 No. 66724 passes through Stowmarket with a light engine movement from North Walsham in Norfolk to Harwich Parkeston Quay yard in Essex. This loco was named *Drax Power Station* in 2007.

94 miles from London Liverpool Street is Diss station, which sits in Norfolk but is very close to the Suffolk border. This station only sees half-hourly service from Norwich and London Liverpool Street using loco-hauled 90 sets. A very grubby Abellio Greater Anglia Class 90 No. 90005 arrives at Diss with a service for London Liverpool Street. This loco was named *Vice Admiral Lord Nelson* in 2005.

Abellio Greater Anglia Class 82 DVT No. 82127 arrives into Diss with a service for Norwich.

Above, below and opposite above: On 11 January 2019, this Abellio Greater Anglia Class 755 FLIRT arrived on its second day of testing on the Great Eastern Main Line. The new bi-mode units, along with new units from Bombardier, are to replace all of Abellio Greater Anglia's new stock starting from May 2019. A FLIRT is a fast light innovative regional train and they are the first of their type to be introduced in the UK. The first one to be tested, No. 755405 is seen arriving into Diss and sitting in the yard before moving the reception siding.

At the other end of the Great Eastern Main Line, 114 miles from London Liverpool Street, is Norwich. The main city of Norfolk, it has six platforms and is where London Liverpool Street services start and finish. In the yard on the left-hand side is recently repainted Class 37 diesel locomotive No. 37409 in British Railways Large Logo blue livery. Two more examples of Class 37s can be seen on the far right-hand side as DRS Class 37 diesel locomotives Nos 37405 and 37558 depart with a short set service for Great Yarmouth. Meanwhile an East Midlands Trains Class 158 Sprinter and Abellio Greater Anglia Class 156 Sprinter can be seen in the background.

Above: Abellio Greater Anglia have one named service – The East Anglian. This is a fast service from Norwich to London Liverpool Street calling only at Diss and Ipswich before heading to London Liverpool Street non-stop, covering the 68 miles in an hour. On 10 February 2019, at a chilly Norwich station, Abellio Greater Anglia Class 90 No. 90012 waits time at Norwich before departing with this service.

Below: From Norwich station passengers are able to transfer to another long-distance service. East Midlands Trains operate a service from Norwich to Liverpool via Nottingham, Manchester and Sheffield, allowing a connection to the Midlands and the North. They operate a fleet of twenty-six Class 158 Sprinters, which cover the 254-mile journey in over five hours. No. 158773 arrives into Norwich after completing this marathon journey. No. 158773 was named Nottingham Eastcroft in 2015 as that is where the 158s are maintained.

Above: Test Trains are a common sight over the UK; different diesel locomotives are used, but most of the time in East Anglia a pair of Class 37 diesel locomotives can be seen operating them. On a late December's evening in 2018, Colas Rail Class 37 No. 37099 sits at Norwich awaiting the route for Great Yarmouth while the crew change ends. No. 37099 used to live on the preserved Gloucester Warwickshire Railway before Colas Rail took ownership.

Below: Class 170 Turbostars are a very common sight at Norwich as three of these units operate the Norwich–Cambridge line every day, but can also be seen working services on the Bittern and Wherry lines to Sheringham and Great Yarmouth. On a summer's evening three Turbostars can be seen parked at Norwich – No. 170206 arriving from Cambridge, No. 170208 awaiting departure for Cambridge and No. 170207 arriving from Sheringham.

When 90 sets encounter issues or aren't needed they can sometimes be found stabled next to the station until they are required for service again. Abellio Greater Anglia Class 90 No. 90002 sits in the yard at Norwich awaiting its next service. This Class 90 is named *Eastern Daily Press 1870–2010 Serving Norfolk for 140 years*. It received this name in 2013.

Norwich station doesn't see much freight anymore and the once large yard next to the station was shrunk down. One freight train that does run to Norwich is the once a week aggregate train from Peak Forest in Derbyshire to Norwich. The unloading point is next to the station, meaning it can be seen being unloaded. This freight diagram is operated by DB and they use a Class 66 diesel locomotive. On 6 February 2019, No. 66151 can be seen shunting around its wagons in the yard.

Every weekday the 17.02 service from London Liverpool Street to Norwich is operated by a twelve-carriage Class 321 EMU. This then forms the 19.30 service back to London Liverpool Street. On the way to Norwich, unlike the usual services, this makes additional calls at Shenfield, Witham and Marks Tey. Due to the many different liveries of 321s, it is quite common to see three different liveries. No. 321326 sits at Norwich before departing for London Liverpool Street.